Math Yellow Pages

for Students and Teachers

from The KIDS' STUFF™ People

Incentive Publications, Inc.
Nashville, TN

Special acknowledgement is accorded to

- *Marjorie Frank and The KIDS' STUFF™
  People for compiling and organizing the
  materials included in this publication*
- *Susan Eaddy for the cover design*
- *Sally Sharpe, Editor*

ISBN 0-86530-008-9
Library of Congress Catalog Card Number 87-82071

TABLE OF CONTENTS

GET YOUR NUMBERS STRAIGHT

Even Numbers--numbers that are divisible by 2

Odd Numbers--numbers that are not even

Prime Number--a number whose only factors are 1 and itself

Composite Numbers--all numbers that are not prime

Whole Number--a member of the set of numbers (0, 1, 2, 3, 4, 5 ...)

Fractional Number--a number that can be named in the form $\frac{a}{b}$ with a and b being any numbers, with the exception that b cannot be 0

Mixed Fractional Number--a number that has a whole number part and a fractional number part

Decimal Number--a number written with a decimal point to express a fraction whose denominator is 10 or a multiple of 10

Mixed Decimal Number--a number that has a whole number part and a decimal number part

Integers--the set of numbers (1, 2, 3 ..., -1, -2, -3 ...), and 0

Positive Integers--on a number line, all the numbers to the right of 0

Negative Integers--on a number line, all the numbers to the left of 0

Rational Numbers--numbers that can be written as a ratio $\frac{a}{b}$ where both a and b are integers and b is not 0 (all integers and decimals that repeat or terminate)

Irrational Numbers--a number than cannot be written as a quotient of two integers (decimals that neither repeat nor terminate)

Real Numbers--rational and irrational numbers together are the set of real numbers

Opposite Numbers--two numbers that are the same distance from 0 but are on opposite sides of 0 (3 is the opposite of -3)

Exponential Numbers--a number with an exponent (An exponent is a number written next to a base number to show how many times the base is to be used as a factor.)

Digit--one number in a numeral that holds a particular place

Significant Digit--all non-zero digits and zero when it has a non-zero digit to the left of it (4.03, not 0.66)

IMPORTANT PROPERTIES

Commutative Property For Addition--the order in which numbers are added does not affect the sum

$$6 + 4 = 4 + 6$$

Commutative Property For Multiplication--the order in which numbers are multiplied does not affect the product

$$8 \times 3 = 3 \times 8$$

Associative Property For Addition--the way in which numbers are grouped does not affect the sum

$$7 + (3 + 2) = (7 + 3) + 2$$

Associative Property For Multiplication--the way in which numbers are grouped does not affect the product

$$(5 \times 2) \times 4 = 5 \times (2 \times 4)$$

Distributive Property--to multiply a sum of numbers, one may first add the numbers in parentheses and then multiply the sum

$$4 \times (6 + 3) = 4 \times 9 = 36$$

or one may multiply the numbers separately and then add the products.

$$4 \times (6 + 3) = (4 \times 6) + (4 \times 3) = 24 + 12 = 36$$

Identity Property For Addition--the sum of 0 and any number is that number

$$7 + 0 = 7 \qquad 486 + 0 = 486$$

Identity Property For Multiplication--the product of 1 and any number is that number

$$9 \times 1 = 9 \qquad 5840 \times 1 = 5840$$

Opposites Property--if the sum of two numbers is 0, then each number is the opposite of the other

$$-4 \text{ is the opposite of } + 4 \text{ because } -4 + (+4) = 0$$

Equation Properties--when adding or subtracting the same number or multiplying or dividing by the same number on both sides of an equation, the result is still an equation

$$n - 6 = 7$$
$$n - 6 + 3 = 7 + 3$$
$$n = 13$$

$$4n = 24$$
$$(4n) \times 3 = 24 \times 3$$
$$n = 6$$

MATH TOOLS, TREASURES, AND TIDBITS

The following items are handy "tools" for math activities.

abacus
alarm clock
attribute blocks
attribute cards

balance

calculator
calculator paper
calipers
cash register
chalkboard compass
compasses
computer
counting rods

egg timers

funnels

geoboards
geometric plane figures
geometric space figures
globe
graduated beakers
grids

maps
mathematics glossary
matrix charts
measuring containers
measuring cups
measuring spoons
measuring sticks
measuring tapes
metric scales
mirrors
multibase arithmetic blocks

number lines

odometers

pegboards
pegs
protractors

rulers

scissors
slide rules
spring scales
stopwatch

thermometers
timers

world atlas

Below is a listing of helpful math "treasures and tidbits" to use in activities, problem solving, displays, etc.

advertisements

bags
bank books
beads
beans
blocks
bottle caps
bottles
bowls
boxes
buttons

cans
carpet scraps
catalogs
checkers
checks
clothespins
coins
containers
cookbooks
counters
cubes

deposit slips
dice
dotted paper

egg cartons

fabric scraps
flashcards
fraction charts

game books
games
geoboard activities
geometric patterns
graph paper

jars
"junk" to measure and compare

magazines
marbles

newspapers

origami paper

paper money
paper plates
pennies
pictures
pipe cleaners
Popsicle sticks
posters
puzzles

recipes
rope
rubber bands

seeds
stamps
straws
string

tangrams
tongue depressors
toothpicks

wallpaper scraps
window shades
wood scraps

yarn

Have a treasure hunt to gather other good math materials! Search in:

drawers and cupboards
kitchens
basements
garage sales

laundry rooms
toy chests
wastebaskets
wallpaper stores

SKILLS THAT MAKE A MATH WHIZ

Skills Checklist For The Primary Grades

Numeration

____ Recognizing that numerals name numbers
____ Associating word names with their corresponding numerals
____ Reading and writing one-digit through six-digit numerals
____ Associating numerals with intervals along a number line
____ Identifying place value for one, two, and three-digit numerals
____ Identifying place value for four, five, and six-digit numerals
____ Identifying place value for millions
____ Expressing numerals up to seven places in expanded notation
____ Renaming tens as ones
____ Renaming hundreds as tens
____ Renaming thousands as hundreds
____ Renaming ten thousands as thousands, hundred thousands as ten thousands, and millions as hundred thousands
____ Reading and expressing numerals using an abacus
____ Distinguishing between numerals having the same digits in different places
____ Identifying positive and negative integers
____ Reading and writing Roman numerals
____ Devising an original numeration system based on 10
____ Experimenting with a non-decimal based numeration system
____ Reading and writing large numbers: millions, billions, trillions
____ Reading exponential numbers

Sets

____ Classifying objects into sets
____ Associating numerals and names with sets of numbers
____ Writing numerals to correspond with sets
____ Associating 0 with any empty set
____ Separating sets into subsets
____ Grouping items into sets of 2, 5, and 10
____ Given two sets, identifying which is greater and which is less
____ Identifying equivalent sets
____ Identifying non-equivalent sets
____ Arranging sets in order of size
____ Finding the union of two or more sets

Number Concepts

____ Identifying even and odd numbers
____ Identifying prime and composite numbers
____ Ordering whole numbers
____ Putting positive and negative integers in order
____ Recognizing ordinal positions (first through tenth)
____ Recognizing a whole as greater than any of its parts
____ Understanding the value of 0

___ Understanding and using the concept of equality and the symbol =
___ Understanding and using the concept of inequality and the symbol ≠
___ Reading and writing sentences which name a whole number
___ Comparing numbers and identifying which is less and which is greater
___ Reading and writing sentences using the symbols   > <
___ Completing sequences of whole numbers
___ Recognizing number patterns
___ Rounding whole numbers to the nearest 10, 100, and 1,000
___ Rounding whole numbers to the nearest 10,000, 100,000, and 1,000,000

Addition and Subtraction of Whole Numbers

___ Understanding and using the symbols + -
___ Learning sums through 20
___ Learning differences through 20
___ Using the terms addend, sum, and difference
___ Understanding the inverse relationship between addition and subtraction
___ Learning fact families through 20
___ Recognizing 0 as the identity element for addition
___ Using the commutative property for addition
___ Finding the missing addend in addition sentences
___ Using a number line to find sums and differences
___ Using the associative property for addition
___ Adding and subtracting vertically
___ Finding sums and differences with two, three, four, five, and six-digit numerals
___ Estimating sums and differences
___ Checking addition problems with subtraction
___ Checking subtraction problems with addition
___ Adding with renaming
___ Subtracting with renaming
___ Adding long columns of numbers
___ Adding and subtracting with more than six digits
___ Writing related addition and subtraction sentences
___ Solving word problems using addition and subtraction facts

Multiplication and Division of Whole Numbers

___ Grouping objects into equivalent sets
___ Separating objects into equivalent subsets
___ Understanding multiplication as the joining of equivalent sets
___ Understanding multiplication as repeated addition
___ Understanding division as the separation of sets into equivalent subsets
___ Understanding division as repeated subtraction
___ Recognizing the inverse relationship of multiplication and division
___ Writing multiplication sentences for numbers in sets
___ Writing division sentences for numbers in subsets
___ Learning multiplication facts for factors through 10
___ Learning fact families for products through 100
___ Using the terms factor and product

___ Solving multiplication and division problems using the number line
___ Recognizing 1 as the identity element for multiplication
___ Using the commutative property of multiplication
___ Understanding and using the symbols $\times$, $\div$, and $\overline{)}$
___ Discovering the role of 0 in multiplication and division
___ Using the associative property of multiplication
___ Writing and solving word problems using multiplication and division facts through 100
___ Multiplying and dividing by 10 and multiples of 10
___ Identifying factors of a number
___ Identifying prime factors of a number
___ Completing prime factorization using factor trees
___ Finding the GCF (Greatest Common Factor) of two numbers
___ Finding the LCM (Least Common Multiple) of two numbers
___ Estimating products and quotients
___ Multiplying by a one-digit number
___ Multiplying by two, three, and four-digit numbers
___ Using the distributive property of multiplication rather than addition
___ Using multiplication to write exponential numbers in expanded notation
___ Dividing by one-digit divisors
___ Completing division problems that have remainders
___ Using the terms divisor, quotient, and remainder
___ Dividing by two, three, and higher-digit divisors
___ Checking division problems using multiplication
___ Finding averages
___ Determining if numbers are divisible by the numbers 2, 3, 4, 5, and 10

Fractions
___ Identifying halves, fourths, and thirds
___ Recognizing that two halves, three thirds, four fourths, etc. make a whole
___ Using fractions to name parts of sets
___ Identifying the numerator of a fraction and understanding its meaning
___ Identifying the denominator of a fraction and understanding its meaning
___ Reading and writing fractions
___ Adding and subtracting like fractions
___ Finding the least common multiple for the denominators of two unlike fractions
___ Rewriting unlike fractions as like fractions
___ Adding and subtracting unlike fractions
___ Finding the greatest common factor for the numerator and denominator of a fraction
___ Identifying fractions that are not in lowest terms
___ Rewriting a fraction in lowest terms
___ Identifying equivalent fractions
___ Identifying improper fractions
___ Determining which of two fractions is greater or less
___ Putting a group of unlike fractions in order
___ Identifying mixed fractional numerals
___ Rewriting improper fractions as mixed numerals
___ Rewriting mixed numerals as improper fractions

—— Multiplying fractions
—— Dividing fractions using the reciprocal method
—— Dividing mixed numerals
—— Using fractions to name ratios
—— Expressing fractional numerals as decimal numerals

Decimals

—— Using dollar signs and decimal points to write money amounts
—— Adding and subtracting money amounts
—— Multiplying and dividing money amounts
—— Understanding that the decimal system is based on tens
—— Understanding the place value of each place to the right of the decimal point
—— Writing decimal numerals three places to the right of the decimal point
—— Writing decimal numerals more than three places to the right of the decimal point
—— Writing mixed decimal numerals
—— Learning to place the decimal point in products
—— Learning to place the decimal point in quotients
—— Adding, subtracting, multiplying, dividing decimal numerals
—— Expressing decimal numerals as fractions
—— Expressing decimal numerals as percents

Measurement

—— Comparing lengths and sizes
—— Understanding the concepts smaller, larger, greater, less, and more
—— Naming days of the week and months of the year
—— Telling time to the nearest hour and half hour
—— Telling time to the nearest minute and second
—— Knowing the number of seconds in a minute, minutes in an hour, hours in a day, days in a week, days in a month, weeks in a year, etc.
—— Measuring length using English and metric measurements
—— Comparing weights of two or more objects
—— Measuring temperature with Celsius and Fahrenheit thermometers
—— Identifying freezing and boiling points on Celsius and Fahrenheit thermometers
—— Comparing weights of objects
—— Measuring weights using English and metric measurements
—— Using scales to find distances on maps and globes
—— Using a protractor to measure angles
—— Measuring the radii and diameters of circles
—— Finding the perimeters of polygons
—— Finding the areas of rectangles, triangles, and other polygons
—— Finding the circumferences and areas of circles
—— Finding the volumes of space figures
—— Finding the surface areas of space figures
—— Estimating measurements
—— Adding, subtracting, multiplying, and dividing measurements

Geometry

—— Identifying circles, triangles, squares, and rectangles

___ Classifying objects by shape
___ Identifying open and closed figures
___ Identifying and drawing points, line segments, lines, and rays
___ Identifying parallel and perpendicular lines
___ Identifying intersections of lines
___ Understanding and using the term plane
___ Recognizing and naming angles as acute, right, obtuse, and straight
___ Drawing angles
___ Identifying similar and congruent shapes
___ Identifying congruent angles
___ Identifying the parts of a circle: radius, diameter, center, arc, chord, tangent
___ Using a compass to draw circles
___ Constructing parallel and perpendicular lines
___ Constructing a bisector of a line segment and an angle
___ Identifying space figures: cubes, prisms, pyramids, cones, cylinders, spheres
___ Naming and counting faces, edges, and vertices of space figures
___ Drawing space figures
___ Identifying symmetrical figures
___ Recognizing and drawing the slide, flip, and turn of a figure

Graphing

___ Reading and making pictographs, bar, circle, and line graphs
___ Locating objects and points on a grid
___ Graphing ordered pairs of integers
___ Locating positions on the earth's grid

Problem Solving

___ Using pictures and manipulatives to solve problems
___ Writing and solving equations for pictured problems
___ Solving problems using information in graphs
___ Completing number sentences corresponding to word problems
___ Writing and solving equations for word problems
___ Estimating answers to word problems
___ Selecting information that is essential for solving a problem
___ Identifying nonessential information for solving a problem
___ Determining the appropriate operation for solving a problem
___ Choosing a method for solving a problem
___ Solving word problems involving more than one step
___ Solving problems involving money
___ Solving problems involving percentages and ratios
___ Predicting outcomes in problem situations
___ Creating word problems

Numeration and Number Concepts

___ Associating word names with corresponding numerals
___ Reading and writing numerals from one to 12 or more digits
___ Identifying place value to billions
___ Expressing numerals in expanded notation
___ Devising an original numeration system
___ Identifying the values of coins and bills
___ Reading and writing Roman numerals
___ Distinguishing between numerals having the same digits in different positions
___ Reading and writing numerals for fractional numbers
___ Reading and writing mixed fractional numbers
___ Reading and writing decimal numerals
___ Expressing fractional numbers in expanded notation
___ Expressing decimal numerals in expanded notation
___ Reading and writing positive and negative integers
___ Reading and writing exponential numbers
___ Reading and writing percentages
___ Comparing and sequencing whole numbers
___ Comparing and sequencing fractional numbers
___ Comparing and sequencing decimal numerals
___ Comparing and sequencing integers
___ Reading and writing sentences using the symbols $<$ $>$
___ Identifying odd and even numbers
___ Identifying prime and composite numbers
___ Understanding the value and properties of 0
___ Rounding whole numbers
___ Rounding fractions
___ Rounding decimals
___ Finding the intersection and union of two sets
___ Forming Cartesian sets
___ Using Venn diagrams to represent sets

Operations With Whole Numbers

___ Learning sums through 20
___ Learning differences through 20
___ Recognizing the inverse relationship between addition and subtraction
___ Using the terms addend, difference, and sum
___ Recognizing 0 as the identity element for addition
___ Using the commutative property for addition
___ Using the associative property for addition
___ Finding the missing addend in number sentences
___ Adding long columns
___ Renaming places up to millions
___ Estimating sums and differences
___ Adding and subtracting up to 12 digits

___ Understanding multiplication as the joining of equivalent sets
___ Understanding multiplication as repeated addition
___ Understanding division as the separation of sets into equivalent subsets
___ Understanding division as repeated subtraction
___ Recognizing the inverse relationship between multiplication and division
___ Learning multiplication and division facts using factors through 20
___ Using the terms factor, product, quotient, division, and remainder
___ Identifying the factors of a whole number
___ Identifying common factors of whole numbers
___ Identifying the greatest common factor of two or more whole numbers
___ Giving the multiples of a whole number
___ Identifying common multiples of whole numbers
___ Identifying the least common multiple of two or more whole numbers
___ Supplying missing factors in multiplication and division problems
___ Discovering the role of 0 in multiplication and division
___ Identifying 1 as the identity element for multiplication or division
___ Using the associative property for multiplication
___ Multiplying and dividing by 10 and multiples of 10
___ Estimating products and quotients
___ Multiplying several digits by one, two, three, four and five-digit numbers
___ Dividing several digits by one, two, three, four and five-digit divisors
___ Checking division problems using multiplication
___ Checking multiplication by casting out nines
___ Finding averages
___ Determining if whole numbers are divisible by the numbers 2, 3, 4, 5, 6, 9, and 10

Fractions and Decimals
___ Identifying fractional parts
___ Using fractions to name parts of sets
___ Identifying the numerator and denominator of fractions
___ Identifying like fractions
___ Adding and subtracting like fractions
___ Identifying equivalent fractions
___ Finding the greatest common factor for the numerator and denominator of a fraction
___ Identifying non-equivalent fractions
___ Identifying improper fractions
___ Identifying mixed numerals
___ Expressing fractions in lowest terms
___ Expressing improper fractions as mixed numerals
___ Expressing mixed numerals as improper fractions
___ Finding the least common multiple for the denominators of two or more fractions
___ Expressing fractions as like fractions
___ Adding and subtracting unlike fractions
___ Adding and subtracting mixed numerals
___ Ordering fractions

___ Multiplying fractions
___ Multiplying and dividing mixed numerals
___ Identifying the reciprocals of fractions
___ Dividing fractions using the reciprocal method
___ Ordering fractions
___ Using dollar signs and decimal points to write money amounts
___ Adding, subtracting, multiplying, and dividing money amounts
___ Writing decimal numerals to the thousandth's place
___ Ordering decimal numerals
___ Expressing fractions as decimal numerals
___ Expressing decimal numerals as fractions
___ Adding, subtracting, multiplying, and dividing decimal numerals
___ Identifying terminating and repeating decimals
___ Estimating sums, differences, products, and dividends with decimals

Ratio, Proportion, and Percent

___ Understanding the meanings of the terms ratio, proportion, and percent
___ Finding ratios
___ Expressing ratios as fractions
___ Expressing ratios as decimals
___ Finding proportions
___ Using cross-multiplication to find ratio
___ Finding percentages
___ Expressing ratios as percentages
___ Using ratio to find equivalent fractions
___ Using ratio to identify similarity
___ Using percent to find discounts, commissions, and interest
___ Finding percent of change

Measurement

___ Estimating measurements
___ Comparing measurements
___ Recognizing and using the following units: inch, foot, yard, mile, millimeter, centimeter, meter, kilometer
___ Recognizing and using the following units: cup, pint, quart, gallon, liter
___ Recognizing and using the following units: ounce, pound, ton, milligram, gram, kilogram, metric ton
___ Measuring length using English and metric measurements
___ Measuring liquid capacity using English and metric measurements
___ Measuring temperatures in Fahrenheit and Celsius
___ Measuring weights using English and metric measurements
___ Finding perimeters of regular and irregular polygons
___ Finding radii, diameters, and circumferences of circles
___ Finding the areas of circles and polygons
___ Finding the capacities of space figures
___ Finding the surface areas of space figures

___ Adding, subtracting, multiplying, and dividing measurements
___ Identifying units of time measurement: seconds, minutes, hours, days, weeks, months, years, decades, and centuries
___ Using a calendar to identify, add, subtract, and count time
___ Telling time on a clock to the minute
___ Recognizing the world's time zones
___ Finding distances on a map
___ Using a map scale to measure and identify distances

Geometry

___ Identifying circles, triangles, rectangles, quadrilaterals, parallelograms, and trapezoids
___ Identifying closed and open figures
___ Identifying and naming line segments
___ Constructing line segments
___ Identifying intersections of lines
___ Identifying and constructing parallel lines
___ Identifying and constructing perpendicular lines
___ Identifying and naming right, obtuse, acute, and straight angles
___ Identifying and defining corresponding angles, complementary angles, and supplementary angles
___ Constructing and measuring angles
___ Recognizing properties of circles, parallelograms, and triangles
___ Identifying congruent shapes
___ Identifying similar figures
___ Identifying the parts of a circle: radius, diameter, center, arc, chord, tangent, circumference
___ Using a compass to draw circles
___ Constructing a bisector for an angle
___ Constructing a bisector for a line segment
___ Constructing equilateral triangles
___ Constructing congruent triangles
___ Identifying cubes, rectangular prisms, triangular prisms, cones, cylinders, pyramids, and spheres
___ Naming and counting the faces, vertices, and edges of space figures
___ Identifying and drawing symmetrical figures
___ Recognizing and drawing the slide of figures
___ Recognizing and drawing the turn of figures
___ Recognizing and drawing the flip of figures

Probability, Statistics, and Graphing

___ Determining odds "in favor"
___ Determining odds "against"
___ Using a ratio to express probability
___ Recording events on a table
___ Recording data on a graph
___ Making predictions
___ Conducting probability experiments

___ Making tree diagrams
___ Determining probability for independent events
___ Determining probability for dependent events
___ Finding range and mean
___ Determining median and mode
___ Reading and making circle graphs
___ Reading and making bar graphs
___ Reading and making line graphs
___ Reading and making pictographs
___ Reading and making histograms
___ Gathering and graphing statistics
___ Graphing ordered pairs
___ Graphing equations
___ Locating points on a four-quadrant grid
___ Graphing solution sets to linear equations
___ Locating positions on the earth's grid

Problem Solving
___ Choosing correct information
___ Eliminating unnecessary information
___ Choosing correct operations
___ Solving multi-step problems
___ Writing an equation to solve a problem

Solving word problems using:
___ All operations with whole numbers
___ All operations with decimals
___ All operations with fractions
___ Rate, time, distance
___ Ratio
___ Percentage
___ Maps
___ Statistics
___ Probability
___ Logic
___ Time
___ Money
___ Measurement
___ Geometry

Pre-Algebra
___ Identifying variables
___ Writing equations
___ Solving equations with one variable
___ Using algebraic formulas for problem solving
___ Writing and evaluating mathematical expressions
___ Solving equations with two variables
___ Using algebraic terms

SPECIAL HOW-TO'S

If you ever find yourself trying to remember how to do a math process, do not worry. Simply turn to this section and locate the appropriate "how-to" process.

HOW TO ROUND A NUMBER

To the nearest ten:

If the ones digit is 5 or more, round to the next highest ten (46 rounds to 50). If the ones digit is less than 5, round to the next lowest ten (43 rounds to 40).

To the nearest hundred:

If the tens digit is 5 or more, round to the next highest hundred (653 rounds to 700). If the tens digit is less than 5, round to the next lowest hundred (638 rounds to 600).

To the nearest thousand:

If the hundreds digit is 5 or more, round to the next highest thousand (4,804 rounds to 5,000). If the hundreds digit is less than 5, round to the next lowest thousand (4,204 rounds to 4,000).

HOW TO FIND AN AVERAGE

To find the average of several numbers, add them together and then divide the sum by the number of numbers.

$$\text{The average of } 12, 46, 75, 94, 101, \text{ and } 38 =$$
$$(12 + 46 + 75 + 94 + 101 + 38) \div 6$$
$$366 \div 6 = 61$$

HOW TO TELL IF A NUMBER IS DIVISIBLE BY 2, 3, 4, 5, 6, 8, 9, or 10

A number is divisible by 2 if the last digit is 0, 2, 4, 6, or 8.
A number is divisible by 3 if the sum of its digits is divisible by 3.
A number is divisible by 4 if the last two digits are divisible by 4.
A number is divisible by 5 if the last digit is 0 or 5.
A number is divisible by 6 if the number is divisible by both 2 and 3.
A number is divisible by 8 if the last three digits are divisible by 8.
A number is divisible by 9 if the sum of its digits is divisible by 9.
A number is divisible by 10 if the last digit is 0.

HOW TO TELL WHICH OF TWO FRACTIONS IS LESS OR GREATER

Cross multiply the two fractions.

1. Multiply 2 x 9   2. Multiply 3 x 7

If the first multiplication has the larger product, the first fraction is greater.

If the second multiplication has the larger product, the second fraction is greater.

In this example, 18 is less than 21. Therefore, $\frac{2}{3} < \frac{7}{9}$.

HOW TO TELL IF TWO FRACTIONS ARE EQUIVALENT

Cross multiply the fractions. If both products are the same, the fractions are equivalent.

$\frac{5}{6} \approx \frac{15}{18}$ 5 x 18 = 90
         6 x 15 = 90

$\frac{2}{3} \neq \frac{5}{7}$ 2 x 7 = 14
         3 x 5 = 15

HOW TO FIND PRIME FACTORS

Write every factor of a number. Continue finding the factors of each factor until you have only prime numbers. A factor tree will help.

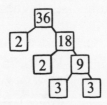

HOW TO FIND THE LEAST COMMON MULTIPLE OF TWO NUMBERS

Write several multiples for each number. Look for the smallest number that is common to both numbers.

For 5 and 9, 45 is the least common multiple.

HOW TO FIND THE LEAST COMMON DENOMINATOR OF TWO FRACTIONS

Find the least common multiple of the two denominators.

For $\frac{7}{8}$ and $\frac{2}{5}$, 40 is the least common denominator.

HOW TO FIND THE GREATEST COMMON FACTOR OF TWO NUMBERS

Write the factors for each number. Find the greatest factor that is common to both numbers.

The factors of 4 are 1, 2, and 4. The factors of 16 are 1, 2, 4, 8, and 16.
1, 2, and 4 are common factors — 4 is the greatest common factor.

HOW TO CHANGE UNLIKE FRACTIONS INTO LIKE FRACTIONS

Find the least common multiple of both denominators. Remember the number you multiply each denominator by in order to get the least common multiple. Then, multiply each numerator by that number.

For $\frac{2}{3}$ and $\frac{4}{5}$, 15 is the least common multiple.

For $\frac{2}{3}$, you must multiply the denominator by 5 to get 15. So, multiply both the numerator and denominator of $\frac{2}{3}$ by 5. ($\frac{2}{3}$ x $\frac{5}{5}$ = $\frac{10}{15}$)

For $\frac{4}{5}$, you must multiply the denominator by 3 to get 15. So, multiply both the numerator and denominator of $\frac{4}{5}$ by 3. ($\frac{4}{5}$ x $\frac{3}{3}$ = $\frac{12}{15}$)

HOW TO ADD OR SUBTRACT FRACTIONS

If the fractions have like denominators, just add or subtract the numerators (denominators stay the same).

If the fractions have unlike denominators, change the fractions into like fractions and then add or subtract.

$$\frac{2}{7} + \frac{1}{2} = \frac{4}{14} + \frac{7}{14} = \frac{11}{14}$$

HOW TO REDUCE A FRACTION TO LOWEST TERMS

Find the greatest common factor and divide both the numerator and denominator by that number.

$\frac{24}{30}$ reduces to $\frac{4}{5}$ when both numerator and denominator are divided by 6.

HOW TO MULTIPLY FRACTIONS

Multiply the numerators to get the numerator of the product and multiply the denominators to get the denominator of the product.

$$\frac{4}{9} \times \frac{2}{11} = \frac{8}{99}$$

HOW TO DIVIDE FRACTIONS

To divide a fraction by another fraction, multiply the fraction by the reciprocal of the divisor.

To divide $\frac{3}{10}$ by $\frac{2}{5}$, simply turn $\frac{2}{5}$ upside down and multiply!

$$\frac{3}{10} \times \frac{5}{2} = \frac{15}{20} = \frac{3}{4}$$

HOW TO CHANGE A FRACTION TO A DECIMAL

Divide the numerator by the denominator.
$$\frac{2}{3} = \begin{array}{r} .6666 \\ 3\overline{)2.0000} \end{array}$$

HOW TO CHANGE A DECIMAL TO A FRACTION

Remove the decimal point and write the number as the numerator. The denominator is 10 or a multiple of 10, depending on what place the last digit of the decimal occupied. For instance, in .355, the last digit is a thousandth.

First, write the fraction. $\frac{355}{1,000}$

Then, reduce the fraction to lowest terms. $\frac{71}{200}$

HOW TO CHANGE A FRACTION TO A PERCENTAGE

Divide the numerator by the denominator. Move the decimal point two places to the right.
$$\frac{3}{10} = \begin{array}{r} .30 \\ 10\overline{)3.00} \end{array} = 30\%$$

HOW TO CHANGE A DECIMAL TO A PERCENTAGE

Move the decimal point two places to the right. $0.465 = 46.5\%$

HOW TO FIND PERCENTAGE

To tell what percentage one number is of a second number, divide the first number by the second. Move the decimal point two places to the right. For example, to find what percentage 5 is of 20, divide 5 by 20.

$$\begin{array}{r} .25 \\ 20\overline{)5.00} \end{array} = 25\%$$

HOW TO FIND SIMPLE INTEREST

Interest = Principal x Interest Rate x Time

Principal = the amount of money you borrow, loan, or deposit
Interest Rate = the percentage of the principal earned in a certain time
Time = the time period in which interest is figured

If you deposit $50 (principal) at 8% interest a year and leave it for three years, you will earn $12.00.

HOW TO FIND PROBABILITY

The probability of something happening is:

$$\frac{1}{\text{the number of possible outcomes}}$$

HOW TO BISECT AN ANGLE

1. Place the point of a compass on point B. Draw an arc intersecting $\overline{BA}$ at X and $\overline{BC}$ at Y.

2. Use X and Y as the centers for two circles, and make the radius of each greater than half the distance between X and Y. Draw arcs intersecting at point Z.

3. Draw ray BZ. Now there are two congruent angles, $\angle$ ABZ and $\angle$ ZBC. Ray BZ is the bisector of $\angle$ ABC.

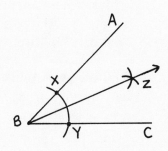

HOW TO BISECT A LINE SEGMENT

1. Open a compass to a radius larger than half of the line segment you wish to bisect (here $\overline{FG}$).

2. Use points F and G as centers and draw arcs that intersect above and below the line segment (here they intersect at points S and T).

3. Draw a line which connects these two points of intersection (see $\overline{ST}$). Point 0 is the midpoint of $\overline{FG}$, and thus $\overline{ST}$ is a perpendicular bisector of $\overline{FG}$.

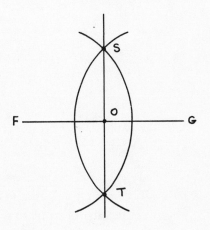

HOW TO TELL IF TWO TRIANGLES ARE CONGRUENT

Two triangles are congruent if one of the following is true.

1. Three sides of one triangle are congruent to three sides of the other triangle.

2. Two sides and the angle between them of one triangle are congruent to two sides and the angle between them of the other triangle.

3. Two angles and the side between them of one triangle are congruent to two angles and the side between them of the other triangle.

HOW TO FIND THE LENGTH OF THE HYPOTENUSE IN A RIGHT TRIANGLE

Use the Pythagorean theorem which gives the formula that the square of the hypotenuse is equal to the squares of the other two sides.

$c^2 = a^2 + b^2$

$c^2 = 6^2 + 8^2$
$c^2 = 36 + 64$
$c^2 = 100$
$c = 10$

23

HOW TO MAKE YOUR OWN TANGRAM PUZZLE

Chinese mathematicians invented a puzzle made from seven pieces. The puzzle pieces form a square, but the pieces may be fitted together to make many shapes. You can create different "pictures" by fitting the tans (tangram pieces) together.

This puzzle is 8cm x 8cm. You can enlarge it by copying it onto a larger grid.

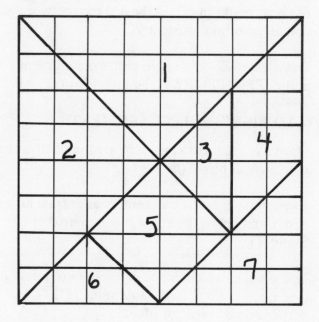

Try making some of these shapes using some or all of the pieces.

The puzzle may also be used to figure areas of shapes. Can you find the area (without measuring) of each of the tangram pieces and each of the shapes you've made?

ALL KINDS OF FORMULAS

PERIMETER

$P = a + b + c$	Perimeter of a triangle
$P = 2 (h + w)$	Perimeter of a rectangle
$C = 2 \pi r$	Circumference of a circle

AREA

$A = \pi r^2$	Area of a circle
$A = s^2$	Area of a square
$A = bh$	Area of a parallelogram
$A = \frac{1}{2} bh$	Area of a triangle
$A = h \left(\frac{b_1 + b_2}{2} \right)$	Area of a trapezoid

VOLUME

$V = Bh$ (B = area of base)	Volume of a rectangular or triangular prism
$V = \frac{1}{3} Bh$ (B = area of base)	Volume of a pyramid
$V = s^3$	Volume of a cube
$V = \pi r^2 h$	Volume of a cylinder
$V = \frac{1}{3} \pi r^2 h$	Volume of a cone
$V = \frac{4}{3} \pi r^3$	Volume of a sphere

WHICH MEASURE?

LENGTH

Metric System

1 centimeter (cm)	=	10 millimeters (mm)
1 decimeter (dm)	=	10 centimeters (cm)
1 meter (m)	=	10 decimeters (dm)
1 meter (m)	=	100 centimeters (cm)
1 meter (m)	=	1000 millimeters (mm)
1 decameter (dkm)	=	10 meters (m)
1 hectometer (hm)	=	100 meters (m)
1 kilometer (km)	=	100 decameters (dkm)
1 kilometer (km)	=	1000 meters (m)

English System

1 foot (ft)	=	12 inches (in)
1 yard (yd)	=	36 inches (in)
1 yard (yd)	=	3 feet (ft)
1 mile (mi)	=	5280 feet (ft)
1 mile (mi)	=	1760 yards (yd)

AREA

Metric System

1 square meter (m^2)	=	100 square decimeters (dm^2)
1 square meter (m^2)	=	10,000 square centimeters (cm^2)
1 hectare (ha)	=	0.01 square kilometer (km^2)
1 hectare (ha)	=	10,000 square meters (m^2)
1 square kilometer (km^2)	=	1,000,000 square meters (m^2)
1 square kilometer (km^2)	=	100 hectares (ha)

English System

1 square foot (ft^2)	=	144 square inches (in^2)
1 square yard (yd^2)	=	9 square feet (ft^2)
1 square yard (yd^2)	=	1296 square inches (in^2)
1 acre (a)	=	4840 square yards (yd^2)
1 acre (a)	=	43,560 square feet (ft^2)
1 square mile (mi^2)	=	640 acres (a)

VOLUME

Metric System

1 cubic decimeter (dm^3)	=	0.001 cubic meter (m^3)
1 cubic decimeter (dm^3)	=	1000 cubic centimeters (cm^3)
1 cubic decimeter (dm^3)	=	1 liter (L)
1 cubic meter (m^3)	=	1,000,000 cubic centimeters (cm^3)
1 cubic meter (m^3)	=	1000 cubic decimeters (dm^3)

English System

1 cubic foot (ft^3)	=	1728 cubic inches (in^3)
1 cubic yard (yd^3)	=	27 cubic feet (ft^3)
1 cubic yard (yd^3)	=	46,656 cubic inches (in^3)

CAPACITY

Metric System
1 teaspoon (t)	=	5 milliliters (mL)
1 tablespoon (T)	=	12.5 milliliters (mL)
1 liter (L)	=	1000 milliliters (mL)
1 liter (L)	=	1000 cubic centimeters (cm^3)
1 liter (L)	=	1 cubic decimeter (dm^3)
1 liter (L)	=	4 metric cups
1 kiloliter (kL)	=	1000 liters (L)

English System
1 tablespoon (T)	=	3 teaspoons (t)
1 cup (c)	=	16 tablespoons (T)
1 cup (c)	=	8 fluid ounces (fl oz)
1 pint (pt)	=	2 cups (c)
1 pint (pt)	=	16 fluid ounces (fl oz)
1 quart (qt)	=	4 cups (c)
1 quart (qt)	=	2 pints (pt)
1 quart (qt)	=	32 fluid ounces (fl oz)
1 gallon (gal)	=	16 cups (c)
1 gallon (gal)	=	8 pints (pt)
1 gallon (gal)	=	4 quarts (qt)
1 gallon (gal)	=	128 fluid ounces (fl oz)

WEIGHT

Metric System
1 gram (g)	=	1000 milligrams (mg)
1 kilogram (kg)	=	1000 grams (g)
1 metric ton (t)	=	1000 kilograms (kg)

English System
1 pound (lb)	=	16 ounces (oz)
1 ton (T)	=	2000 pounds (lb)

TIME

1 minute (min)	=	60 seconds (sec)		1 year (yr)	=	52 weeks
1 hour (hr)	=	60 minutes (min)		1 year (yr)	=	365 or 366 days
1 day	=	24 hours (hr)		1 decade	=	10 years
1 week	=	7 days		1 century	=	100 years

MATHEMATICAL SYMBOLS

$	dollars	=	is equal to
¢	cents	≠	is not equal to
∅	empty set	<	less than
{}	empty set	>	greater than
%	percent	≥	is greater than or equal to
π	pi (3.14159)	≤	is less than or equal to
°	degrees	≐	is approximately equal to
F	Fahrenheit	~	is similar to
C	centigrade	≅	is congruent to
•	point	≇	is not congruent to
√	square root	+4	positive integer
⌒	arc	-4	negative integer
÷	divide	⟷	line
⌐	divide	—	line segment
+	add	→	ray
-	subtract	∠	angle
x	multiply	m∠	measure of angle
•	multiply	△	triangle
∪	union of sets	⊥	perpendicular
∩	intersection of sets	∥	parallel
		a^n	a to the nth power

CAN YOU SPEAK METRIC?

pico	p	one trillionth
nano	n	one billionth
micro	μ	one millionth
milli	m	one thousandth
centi	c	one hundredth
deci	d	one tenth
deka	da	ten
hecto	h	one hundred
kilo	k	one thousand
mega	M	one million
giga	G	one billion
tera	T	one trillion

CONVERSION TABLES

FROM ENGLISH TO METRIC

English Customary Unit	Approximate Metric Equivalent
inch	2.54 centimeters
foot	30.48 centimeters
yard	.9144 meters
mile	1.609 kilometers
square inch	6.452 square centimeters
square foot	929.03 square centimeters
square yard	.836 square meters
square mile	2.590 square kilometers
acre	4047 square meters
cubic inch	16.387 cubic centimeters
cubic foot	28,317 cubic centimeters
cubic yard	.765 cubic meters
ounce	28.3495 grams
pound	453.59 grams
ton	907.18 kilograms
pint	.4732 liters
quart	.9465 liters
gallon	3.785 liters
bushel	35.2390 liters

METRIC TO ENGLISH

To change centimeters	to inches	multiply by .3937
To change meters	to feet	multiply by 3.2808
To change kilometers	to miles	multiply by .6214
To change liters	to quarts	multiply by 1.0567
To change kilograms	to pounds	multiply by 2.2046
To change metric tons	to tons	multiply by 1.1023

TEMPERATURE CONVERSIONS

To change Fahrenheit to Celsius	subtract 32 and then multiply by $\frac{5}{9}$
To change Celsius to Fahrenheit	multiply by $\frac{9}{5}$ and then add 32

ROOT FOR SQUARES

Table Of Square Roots of Integers from 1 - 100

Number	Square Root	Number	Square Root	Number	Square Root	Number	Square Root
1	1	26	5.099	51	7.141	76	8.718
2	1.414	27	5.196	52	7.211	77	8.775
3	1.732	28	5.292	53	7.280	78	8.832
4	2	29	5.385	54	7.348	79	8.888
5	2.236	30	5.477	55	7.416	80	8.944
6	2.449	31	5.568	56	7.483	81	9
7	2.646	32	5.657	57	7.550	82	9.055
8	2.828	33	5.745	58	7.616	83	9.110
9	3	34	5.831	59	7.681	84	9.165
10	3.162	35	5.916	60	7.746	85	9.220
11	3.317	36	6	61	7.810	86	9.274
12	3.464	37	6.083	62	7.874	87	9.327
13	3.606	38	6.164	63	7.937	88	9.381
14	3.742	39	6.245	64	8	89	9.434
15	3.873	40	6.325	65	8.062	90	9.487
16	4	41	6.403	66	8.124	91	9.539
17	4.123	42	6.481	67	8.185	92	9.592
18	4.243	43	6.557	68	8.246	93	9.644
19	4.359	44	6.633	69	8.307	94	9.695
20	4.472	45	6.708	70	8.367	95	9.747
21	4.583	46	6.782	71	8.426	96	9.798
22	4.690	47	6.856	72	8.485	97	9.849
23	4.796	48	6.928	73	8.544	98	9.899
24	4.899	49	7	74	8.602	99	9.950
25	5	50	7.071	75	8.660	100	10

Table Of Squares of Integers from 1 - 20

Number	Square	Number	Square	Number	Square	Number	Square
1	1	6	36	11	121	16	256
2	4	7	49	12	144	17	289
3	9	8	64	13	169	18	324
4	16	9	81	14	196	19	361
5	25	10	100	15	225	20	400

TRICKS OF THE TRADE

THE 3-DIGIT TRICK

1. Write any three digits. 472

2. Repeat the numbers in the same order to get a six-digit number. 472,472

3. Divide the six-digit number by 13.

$$13 \overline{)472,\!472} \quad \frac{36,\!344}{}$$

4. Divide the resulting number by 11.

$$11 \overline{)36,\!344} \quad \frac{3,\!304}{}$$

5. Divide the resulting number by seven.

$$7 \overline{)3,\!304} \quad \frac{472}{}$$

The final answer will always be the original number. **472**

A FANCY NUMBER PATTERN

Write any four digits, repeating the first digit at the end.

Find the difference between each pair of digits and write each answer below the pair as shown. Always repeat the first digit of each row at the end of that row.

```
2  6  8  9  2
 4  2  1  7  4
  2  1  6  3  2
   1  5  3  1  1
    4  2  2  0  4
     2  0  2  4  2
      2  2  2  2  2
```

Continue in this manner until you get a row of the same numbers. It will work every time with any group of numbers!

GOLDBACH'S GUESSES

A man named Christian Goldbach made these two "guesses" (theories) in 1742. No one has been able to prove that either is *always* true, but no one has ever found a case in which either is false. Experiment with them on your own!

Every even number greater than 2 is the sum of two prime numbers.

$$6 = 1 + 5$$

Every odd number greater than 7 is the sum of three prime numbers.

$$17 = 5 + 5 + 7$$

THE REAPPEARING NUMBER TRICK

Try this "trick" on friends. Ask a friend to choose any four digits and follow these directions. The same number will appear every time.

1. Choose four digits from 0 to 9.

3948	1572

2. Arrange the numbers to make the largest possible number. Arrange the numbers again to make the smallest possible number. Subtract the smaller number from the larger number.

9843	7521
-3489	-1257
6354	6264

6543	6642
-3456	-2466

3. Arrange the individual numbers in the resulting answer to make the largest and smallest possible numbers. Subtract the numbers as before.

3087	4176

8730	7641
- 378	-1467
8352	**6174**

4. Continue the process in the same manner. Eventually you will get the number 6174. Regardless of the four numbers you choose, the number 6174 will always appear!

8532
-2358
6174

THE PALINDROME TRICK

A palindrome is a number that reads the same forward and backward such as 48,784. There's a trick to finding palindromes. Follow the steps below.

Write a number.   597

Reverse the number and add.
Continue this process until
you get a palindrome!

+ 795
1392

1392
+ 2931
4323

4323
+ 3234
7557

32

PASCAL'S TRICKY TRIANGLE

Blaise Pascal, a famous French
mathematician, discovered
this unique triangle.
Look carefully at the
numbers and try to
discover the
secret pattern.

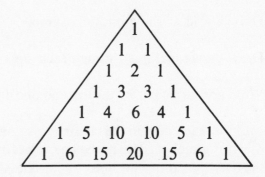

- Add each row across. Notice the pattern of the sums.
- Add each diagonal row from right to left. Notice the pattern of the sums.
- Add each diagonal row from left to right. Notice the pattern of the sums.
  The main secret of the triangle is that each number is the sum of the two numbers above it.

MAGIC SQUARES

Whether adding the rows down, up,
across, or diagonally, all of the sums are
the same in a magic square. After adding
the rows in this magic square, you will
discover that every sum is 15.

8	3	4
1	5	9
6	7	2

Fill in the missing numbers to make each of these a magic square.

5	8	
6	6	6
	4	7

6		6
	7	7
8		8

0	4	8
	6	

Try making your own magic squares!

33

TWO MULTIPLICATION TRICKS

Here's a fun and easy way to work or check multiplication problems.

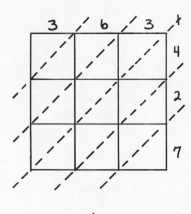

1. Draw a grid as shown in the example.

2. Draw a diagonal line through each square, as shown.

3. Write one factor across the top and one down the right side.

4. Multiply each digit in the factor across the top of the grid by 4, writing each answer in the box beneath the digit. (Write the tens digit above the line and the ones digit below the line as shown.) Now multiply each digit in the top factor by 2, writing each answer in the corresponding box in the second row. Again, multiply the digits in the top factor by 7, writing the answers in the corresponding boxes in the third row.

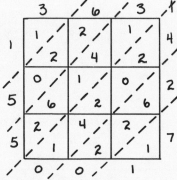

5. Add each diagonal row, beginning with the lower right-hand row. Write the ones digit below the diagonal row and carry the tens digit to the next diagonal row.

Read the product of the two factors starting from the top left-hand corner.

Answer: 155,001

This is another fun way to check multiplication problems.

1. First, work the problem and write the answer.	$3752 \times 1608 = 6,033,216$
2. Then add the digits in each factor.	$3 + 7 + 5 + 2 = 17$ $1 + 6 + 0 + 8 = 15$
3. Now add the digits in each answer of step 2.	$1 + 7 = 8$ $1 + 5 = 6$
4. Multiply the two answers from step 3.	$8 \times 6 = 48$
5. Add the digits in the product. Continue adding the digits in the resulting answers until you get a one-digit answer.	$4 + 8 = 12$ $1 + 2 = 3$
6. Now add the digits in the product of the original problem.	$6 + 0 + 3 + 3 + 2 + 1 + 6 = 21$
7. Continue adding the digits in the resulting answers until you get a one-digit answer.	$2 + 1 = 3$
8. If both one-digit answers (step 5 and step 7) are the same, the product of the problem is correct!	$3 = 3$

COMPUTER-ESE

Computer - an electronic machine which stores instructions and information, deciphers and processes the instructions and information, performs tasks or calculations, and displays the "results" on a screen

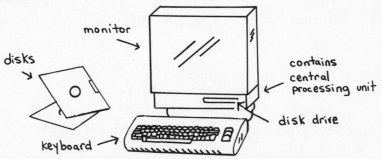

Basic - (Beginner's All-purpose Symbolic Instruction Code) a procedure-oriented computer programming language

Binary - a numbering system based on 2s that uses only two digits, 0 and 1; computers operate on a binary number system

Bit - one electrical signal (or one space that equals no signal) that combines with other bits to make computer codes; a binary digit

Bug - an error in the coding of a computer program

Byte - a term that measures binary digits; 8 or 16 bits

Chip - a tiny electronic component containing thousands of circuits

Cobol - (COmmon Business Oriented Language) a computer programming language

CPU - (Central Processing Unit) the part of the computer that performs logical processes

Data - information put into or received from a computer

Debug - to find and correct errors in a computer program

Disk - a thin, flat, circular metal plate with magnetic material on both sides used to store and read data

Disk Drive - a device in or attached to the computer which reads the information from the disks and stores the information

Floppy Disk - a flexible disk

Fortran - (FORmula TRANslator) a computer programming language used predominantly in science and engineering

Hard Disk - an inflexible disk

Hardware - computer machinery (such as the keyboard, disk drives, monitor, printer, and device containing the CPU)

Input - to enter data and instructions into a computer either manually or with computer input devices other than a keyboard

Interface - a connection between two computer systems or computer devices (such as the keyboard and the monitor or the printer and the computer)

Keyboard - a typewriter-like device with rows of keys which is used to type information into the computer

Memory - a device into which information can be stored

Microcomputer - a small, inexpensive computer system usually used in homes, schools, and small businesses

Modem - a connector that enables computers to talk to each other

Monitor - a screen which displays information

Output - information a computer displays on a screen or prints out after following a set of instructions or completing a task; information stored in memory or a computer file

PC - a personal computer, usually a microcomputer

Pascal - a computer programming language that emphasizes structured programming

Printer - a machine for printing output

Program - instructions given to a computer

Programmer - a person who prepares computer programs

RAM - (Random Access Memory) the part of a computer's memory that contains information which is available to the computer's user

ROM - (Read Only Memory) the part of the computer's memory that stores information needed for the computer to work properly (not available to the user)

Software - computer programs, usually found on disks, tapes, or cards

Terminal - a device for displaying input and output, usually located separately from the computer itself and generally consisting of a keyboard and monitor

MATH TERMS FOR EVERY OCCASION

Absolute Value - the distance a number is from 0 on the number line

Abundant Number - any number for which the sum of its factors (other than the number itself) is greater than itself

Addend - a number being added in an addition problem

In the equation 4 + 7 = 11, 4 and 7 are addends.

Addition - an operation combining two or more numbers

Additive Inverse - for a given number, the number that can be added to give a sum of 0

-4 is the additive inverse of + 4 because - 4 + (+4) = 0

Adjacent Angle - angles that have the same vertex and a common side between them

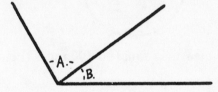

Angle A is adjacent to angle B.

Adjacent Side - the leg next to the given angle in a right triangle

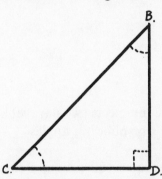

Side $\overline{CD}$ is adjacent to angle C.

Algorithm - a method commonly used for performing computations involving mathematical operations

Altitude of a Triangle - the distance between a point on the base and the vertex of the opposite angle, measured along a line which is perpendicular to the base (the altitude is also referred to as the height of the triangle)

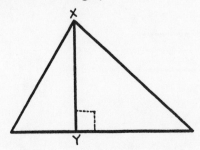

Segment $\overline{XY}$ is the altitude in this triangle.

Angle - a figure formed by two rays having a common endpoint (vertex)

An *acute angle* measures less than 90° (see # 1).

A *right angle* measures 90° (see # 2).

An *obtuse angle* measures more than 90° and less than 180° (See # 3).

A *straight angle* measures 180° (See # 4).

Central Angle - an angle formed by two radii of a circle.

Angle M is a central angle.

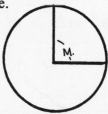

Complementary Angles - two angles whose combined measures equal 90°; X and Y (below) are complementary angles

Congruent Angles - angles having the same measure

Corresponding Angles - angles which are formed when a line intersects two parallel lines; corresponding angles are congruent; B and F (below) are corresponding angles

Supplementary Angles - two angles whose combined measures equal 180°; A and B (below) are supplementary angles

Vertical Angles - angles which are formed opposite one another when two lines intersect; vertical angles are congruent; E and H (below) are vertical angles

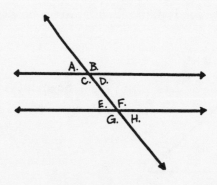

Arc - a part of a circle between any two points on the circle

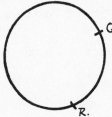

Segment $\overset{\frown}{QR}$ is an arc.

Area - the measure of the region inside a closed plane figure; area is measured in square units

Associative Property For Addition and Multiplication - the rule stating that the grouping of addends or factors does not affect the sum or product

$(3 + 6) + 9 = 3 + (6 + 9)$ $\qquad\qquad$ $(2 \times 4) \times 7 = 2 \times (4 \times 7)$

Average - the sum of a set of numbers divided by the number of addends

The average of 1, 2, 7, 3, 8, and $9 = \dfrac{1 + 2 + 7 + 3 + 8 + 9}{6} = 5$

Axes - two perpendicular number lines with a common origin

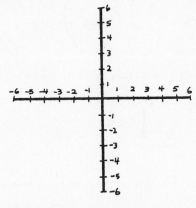

Axis - a number line which may be vertical or horizontal

Base - 1. a side of a geometric figure 2. a standard grouping of a numeration system

If a numeration system groups objects by fives, it is called a base 5 system (23 is a base 5 numeral meaning two fives and three ones).

Binary Operation - any operation involving two numbers

Bisect - to divide into two congruent parts

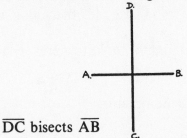

$\overline{DC}$ bisects $\overline{AB}$

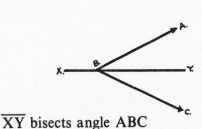

$\overline{XY}$ bisects angle ABC

Bisector - a line or ray that divides a segment or angle into two congruent parts

Capacity - the measure of the amount that a container will hold

Cardinal Number - the number of elements in a set

Cartesian Set - a set resulting from the pairing of members of two other sets

Chance - the probability or likelihood of an occurrence

Chord - a line segment having endpoints on a circle

$\overline{XY}$ is a chord.

Circle - a closed curve in which all points on the edge are equidistant from a given point in the same plane

Circumference - the distance around a cricle

circumference = π x diameter

Closed figure - a set of points that encloses a region in the same plane; a curve that begins and ends at the same point

Coefficient - in the expression 8x, 8 is the coefficient of x

Coincide - two lines coincide when they intersect at more than one point

Collinear - when points are on the same line, they are collinear

Commission - an amount of money earned for selling a product or for providing a service

Common Denominator - a whole number that is the denominator for both members of a pair of fractions

For $\frac{3}{7}$ and $\frac{5}{7}$, 7 is a common denominator.

Common Factor - a whole number which is a factor of two or more numbers (3 is a factor common to 6, 9, and 12)

Common Multiple - a whole number that is a multiple of two or more numbers (12 is a multiple common to 2, 3, 4, and 6)

Commutative Property for Addition and Multiplication - the rule stating that the order of addends or factors has no effect on the sum or product

$$3 + 9 = 9 + 3 \text{ and } 4 \times 7 = 7 \times 4$$

Compass - a tool for drawing circles

Complex Fraction - a fraction having a fraction or a mixed numeral as its numerator and/or denominator

$$\frac{\frac{2}{5}}{\frac{1}{3}}$$

Composite Number - a number having at least one whole number factor other than 1 and itself

Cone - a space figure with a circular base and a vertex

Congruent - of equal size; the symbol $\cong$ means congruent

Triangles ABC and
DEF are congruent.

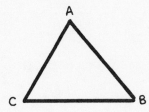 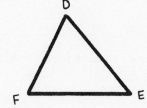

Coordinate plane - a grid on a plane with two perpendicular lines of axes

Coordinates - a pair of numbers which give the location of a point on a plane

Coplanar - when lines or points are in the same plane, they are coplanar

Cosine - the ratio between the hypotenuse and the adjacent side to a given acute angle in a right triangle

Cross Product Method - means of testing for equivalent fractions

$$\text{If } \frac{3}{5} = \frac{6}{10}, \text{ then } 3 \times 10 \text{ will equal } 5 \times 6.$$

Cube - a space figure having six congruent, square faces

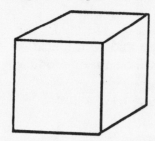

Cube Numeration - a number raised to the third power (8^3)

Curve - a set of points connected by a line segment

Customary units - units of the measurement system commonly used in a given country (inches, feet, pounds, ounces, and miles are customary units in the U.S.)

Cylinder - a space figure having two congruent, circular bases

Data - figures, facts or information

Decagon - a ten-sided polygon

Decimal Numeral - a name for a fractional number expressed with a decimal point, such as .27 (4.03 is a mixed decimal)

Decimal System - a numeration system based on grouping by tens

Degree - 1. a unit of measure used in measuring angles (a circle contains 360 degrees) 2. a unit for measuring temperature

Denominator - the bottom number in a fraction; the denominator tells how many parts there are in a whole unit

Diagonal - a line segment joining two nonadjacent vertices in a polygon

$\overline{AC}$ is a diagonal in this figure.

Diameter - a line segment which has its endpoints on a circle and which passes through the center of the circle

$\overline{LM}$ is the diameter
of this circle.

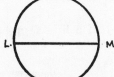

Difference - 1. the distance between two numbers on the number line 2. the result of subtracting the lesser from the greater

In the equation 99 - 46 = 53, 53 is the difference.

Digit - a symbol used to write numerals; in the decimal system, there are ten digits (0-9)

Disjoint Sets - sets having no members in common

Distributive Property for Multiplication Over Addition - the rule stating that when the sum of two or more addends is multiplied by another number, each addend must be multiplied separately and then the products must be added together

$$3 \times (4 + 6 + 9) = (3 \times 4) + (3 \times 6) + (3 \times 9)$$

Dividend - a number which is to be divided in a division problem

In the equation $7\overline{)63}$, 63 is the dividend.

Divisibility - a number is divisible by a given number if the quotient of the two numbers is a whole number

189 is divisible by 9 because 189 ÷ 9 is a whole number.

Division - the operation of finding a missing factor when the product and one factor are known

Divisor - the factor used in a division problem for the purpose of finding the missing factor

$$12\overline{)24}^{\,2} \quad \text{The divisor is 12.}$$

Dodecahedron - a space figure with 12 pentagonal faces

43

Edge - a line segment formed by the intersection of two faces of a geometric space figure

Elements - the members of a set

Empty Set - a set having no elements, also called a null set

$$\{\ \} \text{ or } \emptyset \text{ represents an empty set.}$$

Endpoint - a point at the end of a line segment or ray

G is the endpoint of
this ray.

Equation - a mathematical sentence which states that two expressions are equal

$$7 \times 9 = 3 + (4 \times 15)$$

Equator - an imaginary line at 0 degrees latitude on the earth's grid

Equilateral - having sides of the same length

Figure ABC is an equilateral
triangle. All of its sides
are the same length.

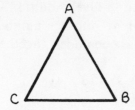

Equivalent Fractions - fractions that name the same fractional number

$$\frac{3}{4} \text{ and } \frac{9}{12} \text{ are equivalent.}$$

Equivalent Sets - sets having the same number of members

Estimate - an approximation or rough calculation

Even Number - one of the set of whole numbers having the number 2 as a factor

Expanded Notation - the method of writing a numeral to show the value of each digit

$$5327 = 5000 + 300 + 20 + 7$$

Exponent - a numeral telling how many times a number is to be used as a factor

In 6^3, the exponent is 3. $6^3 = 6 \times 6 \times 6 = 216$

Face - a plane region serving as a side of a space figure

Factor - one of two or more numbers that can be multiplied to find a product

In the equation 6 × 9 = 54, 6 and 9 are factors.

Factor Tree - a pictorial means of showing the factors of a number

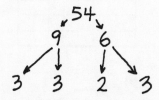

Finite Set - a set having a specific number of elements

$$\{2, 5, 9, 15\} \quad \text{is a finite set.}$$

Flip - to "turn over" a geometric figure; the size or shape of the figure does not change

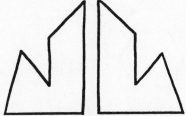

Flow Chart - a diagram that gives instructions in a certain order

Fraction - the name for a fractional number written in the form $\frac{a}{b}$; a is the numerator, b is the denominator

Fractional Number - a number that can be named as a fraction, $\frac{a}{b}$; the numerator and denominator can be any numbers with the exception that the denominator cannot be 0

Frequency - the number of times a given item occurs in a set of data

Frequency Graph - a way to organize and picture data using a grid

Frequency Table - data arranged on a table to show how often events occur

Function - a set of ordered pairs of numbers which follow a function rule and in which no two first numbers are the same

$$\{ (2,5) \ (3,6) \ (4,7) \ (5,8) \ (6,9) \} \text{The rule for this set is to add one.}$$

Geometry - the study of space and figures in space

Gram - a standard unit for measuring mass in the metric system

45

Graph - a drawing showing relationships between sets of numbers

Greatest Common Factor - the largest number that is a factor of two other numbers (6 is the greatest common factor of 18 and 24)

Grid - a set of horizontal and vertical lines spaced uniformly

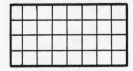

Hemisphere - half of a sphere

Heptagon - a seven-sided polygon

Hexagon - a six-sided polygon

Horizontal - a line that runs parallel to a base line

Line $\overleftrightarrow{GH}$ is a horizontal line.

Hypotenuse - the longest side of a right triangle located opposite the right angle

Side $\overline{OP}$ is the hypotenuse of this triangle.

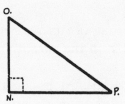

Icosahedron - a space figure with 20 faces

Identity Element For Addition - 0 is the identity element for addition because any number plus 0 equals that number

$$(3 + 0 = 3)$$

Identity Element For Multiplication - the number 1 is the identity element for multiplication because any number multiplied by 1 equals that number

$$(17 \times 1 = 17)$$

Improper Fraction - a fraction having a numerator equal to or greater than the denominator, therefore naming a number of 1 or more

$$\frac{9}{4} \text{ is an improper fraction.}$$

Inequality - a number sentence showing that two groups of numbers stand for different numbers

The signs $\neq$, $<$, and $>$ show inequality. $7 + 5 \neq 12 - 9$

Infinite Set - a set having an unlimited number of members

Integer - any member of the set of positive or negative counting numbers and 0

$$(\ldots -4, -3, -2, -1, 0, 1, 2, 3, 4, \ldots)$$

Interest - an amount of money earned from a loan or a deposit

Intersection of Lines - the point at which two lines meet

Lines $\overleftrightarrow{AB}$ and $\overleftrightarrow{CD}$
intersect at
point Y.

Intersection of Planes - a line formed by the set of points at which two planes meet

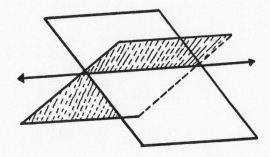

Intersection of Sets - the set of members common to each of two or more sets

The intersection of these sets is
3, 7, and 8. The symbol $\cap$ represents
intersection.

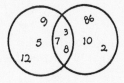

Inverse - opposite; addition and subtraction are inverse operations and multiplication is the inverse of division

Irrational Number - a decimal that neither terminates or repeats

Lateral Faces - the plane surfaces of a space figure which are not bases

The lateral faces of this
triangular prism are shaded.

Latitude - the distance, measured in degrees, north or south of the equator; lines of latitude run parallel to the equator

Least Common Denominator - the smallest whole number which is a multiple of the denominators of two or more fractions

The least common denominator for $\frac{1}{3}$ and $\frac{3}{4}$ is 12.

Least Common Multiple - the smallest whole number which is divisible by each of two or more given numbers

The least common multiple of 2, 6, 9, and 18 is 18.

Legs - sides adjacent to the right angle in a right triangle

$\overline{QP}$ and $\overline{QR}$ are legs
in this triangle.

Like Fractions - fractions having the same denominator

$$\frac{2}{9} \text{ and } \frac{12}{9} \text{ are like fractions.}$$

Line - one of the four undefined terms of geometry used to define all other terms

Line of Reflection - the Y-axis in a number plane

Line of Symmetry - a line on which a figure can be folded so that the two parts are exactly the same

Line $\overleftrightarrow{ST}$ is the line of
symmetry in this figure.

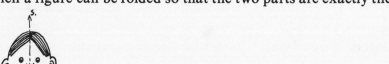

Line Segment - part of a line consisting of a path between two endpoints

$\overline{AB}$ and $\overline{CD}$ are line segments.

Linear Measure (or length) - the measure of distance between two points along a line

Liter - a metric system unit of measurement for liquid capacity

Logic - principles of reasoning

Longitude - the distance, measured in degrees, east or west of the prime meridian; lines of longitude run north and south on the earth's grid, meeting at the poles

Lowest Terms - when a fraction has a numerator and denominator with no common factor greater than 1, the fraction is in lowest terms

$$\frac{3}{7}$$ is a fraction in lowest terms.

Mean - average; the sum of numbers in a set divided by the number of addends

The mean of 6, 8, 9, 19, and 38 is $\frac{80}{5}$ or 16.

Measurement - the process of finding the length, area, capacity, or amount of something

Median - the middle number in a set of numbers; the median is determined by arranging numbers in order from lowest to highest and by counting to the middle

The median of (3, 8, 12, 17, 20, 23, 27) is 17.

Median of a Trapezoid - the line segment joining the midpoints of the nonparallel sides of a trapezoid

Meter - a metric system unit of linear measurement

Metric System - a system of measurement based on the decimal system

Midpoint - a point that divides a line segment into two congruent segments

Point B is the midpoint
of $\overline{DE}$.

Mixed Numeral - a numeral that includes a whole number and a fractional number or a whole number and a decimal

$$7\frac{1}{2}$$ and 37.016 are mixed numerals.

Mode - the score or number found most frequently in a set of numbers

Modular Number System - a number system that uses a limited number of units for counting

Multiple - the product of two whole numbers

Multiplication - an operation involving repeated addition

$$4 \times 5 = 4 + 4 + 4 + 4 + 4$$

Multiplicative Inverse - for any given number, the number that will yield a product of 1

$\frac{4}{3}$ is the multiplicative inverse of $\frac{3}{4}$ because $\frac{4}{3} \times \frac{3}{4} = 1$.

Napier's Bones - an early calculating tool, similar in principle to the slide rule, used for multiplication

Negative Integer - one of a set of counting numbers that is less than 0

Nonagon - a nine-sided polygon

Number - a mathematical idea concerning the amount contained in a set

Number Line - a line which has numbers corresponding to points along it

Numeral - a symbol used to represent or name a number

Numeration System - a system of symbols used to express numbers

Numerator - the number above the line in a fraction

Octagon - an eight-sided polygon

Octahedron - a space figure with eight faces

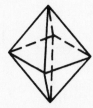

Odd Number - a whole number belonging to the set of numbers equal to (n x 2) + 1

(1, 3, 5, 7, 9 . . .) are odd numbers.

Odds Against - the ratio of the number of unfavorable outcomes to the number of favorable outcomes

Odds in Favor - the ratio of the number of favorable outcomes to the number of unfavorable outcomes

Open Sentence - a number sentence with a variable

Opposite Property - a property which states that if the sum of two numbers is 0, then each number is the opposite of the other

-4 + 4 = 0 ; -4 and 4 are opposites

Ordered Pair - a pair of numbers in a certain order with the order being of significance

Ordinal Number - a number telling the place of an item in an ordered set (sixth, eighth, etc.)

Origin - the beginning point on a number line; the origin is often 0

Outcome - a possible result in a probability experiment

Palindrome - a number which reads the same forward and backward

(343, 87678, 91219, etc.)

Parallel Lines - lines in the same plane which do not intersect

These lines
are parallel.

Parallelogram - a quadrilateral whose opposite sides are parallel

Pentagon - a five-sided polygon

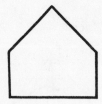

Percent - a comparison of a number with 100

43 compared to 100 is 43%

Perimeter - the distance around the outside of a closed figure

Periods - groups of three digits in numbers

723,301,611

millions period   thousands period   units period

Perpendicular Lines - two lines in the same plane that intersect at right angles

These lines are
perpendicular to
one another.

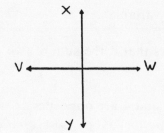

Pi - the ratio of a circle's circumference to its diameter

pi = 3.14159265 (a non-terminating decimal)

The symbol π signifies pi.

Pictograph - a graph that uses pictures or symbols to represent numbers

Place Value - the value assigned to a digit due to its position in a numeral

Plane - one of the four undefined terms of geometry used to define all other terms

Plane Figure - a set of points in the same plane enclosing a region

Figures A and B are plane figures.

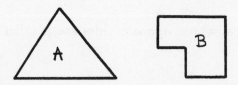

Point - one of the four undefined terms in geometry used to define all other terms

Polygon - a simple, closed plane figure having line segments as sides

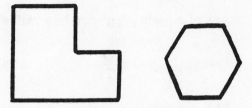

Polyhedron - space figure formed by intersecting plane surfaces called faces

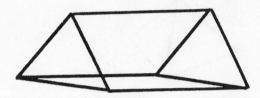

Positive Integer - one of a set of counting numbers that is greater than 0

Prime Factor - a factor that is a prime number

1, 2, and 5 are prime factors of 20

Prime Meridian - an imaginary line on the earth's grid located at 0 longitude which runs north and south through Greenwich, England

Prime Number - a number whose only number factors are 1 and itself

Principal - an amount loaned to someone or deposited in a bank

Prism - a space figure with two parallel, congruent polygonal faces (called bases); a prism is named by the shape of its bases

triangular prism   rectangular prism

Probability - a study of the likelihood that an event will occur

Product - the answer in a multiplication problem

Property of One - a property which states that any number multiplied by 1 will equal that number

Property of Zero - a property which states that any number plus zero equals that number

Proportion - a number statement of equality between two ratios

$$\frac{3}{7} = \frac{9}{21}$$

Protractor - an instrument used for measuring angles

Pyramid - a space figure having one polygonal base and four triangular faces which have a common vertex

Pythagorean Theorem - a proposition stating that the sum of the squares of the two shorter sides of a right triangle is equal to the square of the third side

In triangle ABC,
$\overline{AB}^2 + \overline{BC}^2 = \overline{CA}^2$

Quadrilateral - a four-sided polygon

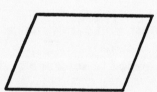

Quotient - the answer in a division problem

Radical Sign - the square root symbol

Radius - a line segment having one endpoint in the center of the circle and another on the circle

$\overline{FG}$ is the radius of
this circle.

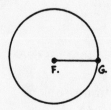

Random - an experiment in which the results are not predictable, even when repeated

Rate - a comparison of two quantities

Ratio - a comparison of two numbers expressed as $\frac{a}{b}$

Rational Numbers - a number that can be written as the quotient of two numbers (a terminating or repeating decimal is rational)

Ray - a portion of a line extending from one endpoint in one direction indefinitely

Real Numbers - any number that is a positive number, a negative number, or 0

Reciprocals - a pair of numbers whose product is one

$$\frac{1}{2} \text{ and } \frac{2}{1} \text{ are reciprocals.}$$

Reciprocal Method For Dividing Fractions - a means of dividing fractions that involves replacing the divisor with its reciprocal and then multiplying

$$\frac{2}{3} \div \frac{4}{7} = \frac{2}{3} \times \frac{7}{4} = \frac{14}{12} = 1\frac{1}{6}$$

Rectangle - a parallelogram having four right angles

Region - the set of all points on a closed curve and in its interior

Relation - a set of ordered pairs

Remainder - the number (less than the divisor) that is left after a division problem is completed

$$\begin{array}{r} 20 \\ 21\overline{)426} \quad\quad 6 = \text{remainder} \\ 420 \\ \hline 6 \end{array}$$

Rename - to name numbers with a different set of numerals

Repeating Decimal - a decimal in which a certain set of digits repeats without end (0.363636)

Replacement Set - a set of numbers which could replace a variable in a number sentence

Rhombus - a parallelogram having congruent sides

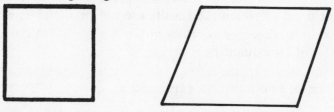

Roman Numerals - numerals used by the Romans for keeping records

Rounding - disregarding all digits in a number beyond a certain significance

Scale Drawing - a drawing of an object with all distances in proportion to the corresponding distances on the actual object

Scientific Notation - a number expressed as a decimal number (usually with an absolute value less than 10) multiplied by a power of 10

$$4.53 \times 10^3 = 4530$$

Segment - two points and all of the points on the line or arc between them

Sequence - a continuous series of numbers ordered according to a pattern

Set - a collection of items called members or elements

Similarity - a property of geometric figures having angles of the same size

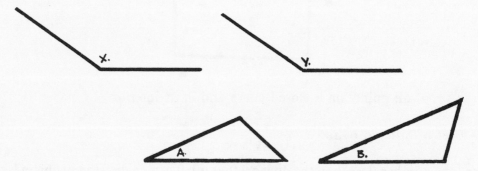

Angles X and Y are similar.   Triangles A and B are similar.

Simple Closed Curve or Figure - a closed curve whose path does not intersect itself

Skew Lines - lines that are not in the same plane and do not intersect

Skip Count - counting by skipping a certain number of digits (counting by 2s, 5s, and 10s, etc.)

Slide - moving a figure without turning or flipping it; the shape or size of a figure is not changed by a slide

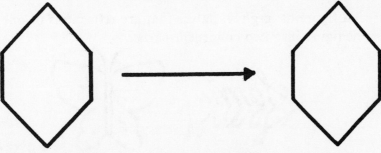

Solution - the number that replaces a variable to complete an equation

Solution Set - the set of possible solutions for a number sentence

Space Figure - a figure which consists of a set of points in two or more planes

Sphere - a space figure formed by a set of points equidistant from a center point

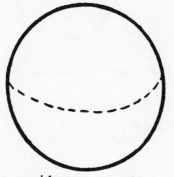

Square - a rectangle with congruent sides

Square Root - a number which yields a given product when multiplied by itself

The square root of 25 is 5 because 5 x 5 = 25.

Statistics - numerical observations or data

Subset - every member of a set, or any combination of the members of a set

Subtraction - the operation of finding a missing addend when one addend and the sum are known

Sum - the answer in an addition problem resulting from the combination of two addends

Surface - a region lying on one plane

Surface Area - the space covered by a plane region or by the faces of a space figure

Symmetric Figure - a figure having two halves that are reflections of one another; a line of symmetry divides the figure into two congruent parts

These figures
are symmetric.

Tangent - a line which touches a curve at only one point

Line $\overleftrightarrow{GH}$ is tangent to the
circle at point X.

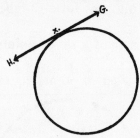

Terminating Decimal - a decimal that shows a quotient of a whole number and a power of 10

$$0.0204 = \frac{204}{10000} \qquad 3.56 = \frac{356}{100}$$

Terms of a Fraction - the numerator and denominator of a fraction

Tetrahedron - a space figure with four triangular faces

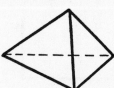

Transversal - a line that intersects two or more parallel lines

$\overleftrightarrow{GH}$ is a transversal of
lines $\overleftrightarrow{AB}$ and $\overleftrightarrow{CD}$.

Trapezoid - a quadrilateral having only two parallel sides

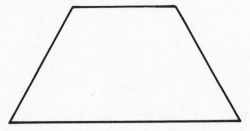

Triangle - a three-sided polygon

    Acute Triangle - a triangle in which all three angles are less than 90°

    Equilateral Triangle - a triangle with three congruent sides and three congruent angles

    Isosceles Triangle - a triangle with at least two congruent sides

    Obtuse Triangle - a triangle having one angle greater than 90°

    Right Triangle - a triangle having one 90° angle

    Scalene Triangle - a triangle in which no two sides are congruent

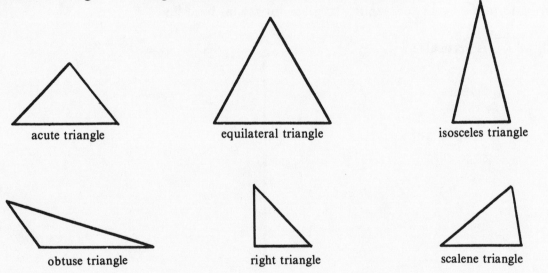

acute triangle   equilateral triangle   isosceles triangle

obtuse triangle   right triangle   scalene triangle

Turn - a move in geometry which involves turning, but not flipping, a figure; the size or shape of a figure is not changed by a turn

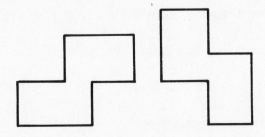

Union of sets - a set containing the combined members of two or more sets; the symbol U represents union

The union of sets
A and B is
(7, 12, 14, 20, 26, and 25).

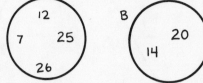

Unit - 1. the first whole number 2. a determined quantity used as a standard for measurement

Variable - a symbol in a number sentence which could be replaced by a number

$$In \ 3 + 9x = 903, \ x \ is \ the \ variable.$$

Venn Diagram - a pictorial means of representing sets and the union or intersection of sets (see example under Union Of Sets)

Vertex - a common endpoint of two rays forming an angle, two line segments forming sides of a polygon, or two planes forming a polyhedron

Point Z is the vertex
of this angle.

Vertical - a line that is perpendicular to a horizontal base line

Line $\overleftrightarrow{KL}$ is vertical.

Volume - the measure of capacity or space enclosed by a space figure

Whole Number - a member of the set of numbers (0, 1, 2, 3, 4 . . .)

X-Axis - the horizontal number line on a coordinate grid

Y-Axis - the vertical number line on a coordinate grid

Zero - the number of members in an empty set

FAST FACTS

Addition & Subtraction Facts Matrix

ADDITION PROBLEM: Locate one addend on the top horizontal row. Locate the second addend on the left-most vertical row. Draw an imaginary line from each number to the box in which the lines meet. The number in that box is the sum of the two addends.

SUBTRACTION PROBLEM: Locate one addend in the top horizontal row. Draw an imaginary line from that number down the page vertically until you come to the number from which you're subtracting. Draw an imaginary line from that number to the left-most box. The number in that box is the missing addend.

+	1	2	3	4	5	6	7	8	9	10	11	12
1	2	3	4	5	6	7	8	9	10	11	12	13
2	3	4	5	6	7	8	9	10	11	12	13	14
3	4	5	6	7	8	9	10	11	12	13	14	15
4	5	6	7	8	9	10	11	12	13	14	15	16
5	6	7	8	9	10	11	12	13	14	15	16	17
6	7	8	9	10	11	12	13	14	15	16	17	18
7	8	9	10	11	12	13	14	15	16	17	18	19
8	9	10	11	12	13	14	15	16	17	18	19	20
9	10	11	12	13	14	15	16	17	18	19	20	21
10	11	12	13	14	15	16	17	18	19	20	21	22
11	12	13	14	15	16	17	18	19	20	21	22	23
12	13	14	15	16	17	18	19	20	21	22	23	24

Multiplication & Division Facts Matrix

MULTIPLICATION PROBLEM: Locate one factor on the top horizontal row and the second on the left-most vertical row. Draw a imaginary line from each number to the box in which the lines meet. The number in that box is the product of the two factors.

DIVISION PROBLEM: Locate the divisor on the top horizontal row. Draw an imaginary line from that number down the page vertically until you come to the number being divided. Draw an imaginary line from that number to the left-most box. The number in that box is the missing factor.

X	1	2	3	4	5	6	7	8	9	10	11	12
1	1	2	3	4	5	6	7	8	9	10	11	12
2	2	4	6	8	10	12	14	16	18	20	22	24
3	3	6	9	12	15	18	21	24	27	30	33	36
4	4	8	12	16	20	24	28	32	36	40	44	48
5	5	10	15	20	25	30	35	40	45	50	55	60
6	6	12	18	24	30	36	42	48	54	60	66	72
7	7	14	21	28	35	42	49	56	63	70	77	84
8	8	16	24	32	40	48	56	64	72	80	88	96
9	9	18	27	36	45	54	63	72	81	90	99	108
10	10	20	30	40	50	60	70	80	90	100	110	120
11	11	22	33	44	55	66	77	88	99	110	121	132
12	12	24	36	48	60	72	84	96	108	120	132	144

NOTES